NATURE'S Yucky!

NATURE'S
Yucky!

Gross Stuff That Helps Nature Work

LEE ANN LANDSTROM & KAREN I. SHRAGG

Illustrated by CONSTANCE R. BERGUM

Mountain Press Publishing Company
Missoula, Montana
2003

Ninth Printing, April 2013

AUTHORS' NOTE

As longtime directors of nature centers, we strive to portray nature in a positive light. Some things about nature can be gross, though, no matter what the reasons are for the actions. We hope that teaching children about the benefits of these yucky behaviors will give young people a greater understanding and appreciation of the amazing natural world.

Library of Congress Cataloging-in-Publication Data

Landstrom, Lee Ann, 1954–
    Nature's yucky! : gross stuff that helps nature work / Lee Ann Landstrom and Karen I. Shragg ; illustrated by Constance R. Bergum. — 1st ed.
        p. cm.
Summary: Relates facts about unusual behaviors exhibited by different animals, and explains the reasons for these actions.
    ISBN 978-0-87842-474-0 (pbk. : alk. paper)
    1. Animals—Food—Juvenile literatue. 2. Eliminative behavior—Juvenile literature. [I. Animals—Miscellanea.] I. Shragg, Karen, 1954– II. Bergum, Constance Rummel, ill. III. title.
    QL756.5.L36   2003
    591.5'3—dc21

                                                              2003004813

PRINTED IN HONG KONG BY MANTEC PRODUCTION COMPANY

MP Mountain Press
PUBLISHING COMPANY
P.O. Box 2399 • Missoula, MT 59806 • 406-728-1900
800-234-5308 • info@mtnpress.com
www.mountain-press.com

Did you know . . .

That MOOSE,

those gangly, goofy-looking mega-deer,

cough up and rechew their half-digested food?

Eeewww!! That's Yucky!

But hey, it's okay.
Just imagine if it weren't that way!

If it weren't that way, moose couldn't digest the plants they eat. This large, hoofed animal is a ruminant. A ruminant has a stomach with four parts. After a moose chews and swallows its leafy food, the food goes into stomachs one and then two for softening. Later, the moose coughs up a slimy, half-digested plant wad called a cud. It chews the cud a while before swallowing it into stomachs three and then four. By double-chewing its food, a moose grinds up the tough leaves and bark, making them easier to digest. Aren't you glad you don't have to cough up and rechew your green beans?

Did you know . . .

That BALD EAGLES,

those elegant, awesome, airborne hunters,

eat rotting, dead fish?

Eeewww!!
That's YUCKY!

But hey, it's okay.

Just imagine if it weren't that way!

If it weren't that way, these fish-eating birds would have to work harder for their food. Bald eagles catch and eat mainly fish but also small mammals and birds. Dead fish do not struggle and are easier for the eagle to find and catch than live animals, so they make an easy meal. Eagles and other animals that eat dead animals are called scavengers. Scavengers recycle the smelly mess of rotting meat and fish leftovers. How would you like rotting fish for your dinner?

Did you know . . .

That HOARY MARMOTS,

those waddling, wide-bodied

woodchuck cousins,

don't poop

all winter long?

Eeewww!! That's Yucky!

But hey, it's okay.

Just imagine if it weren't that way!

If it weren't that way, this rodent couldn't survive winter's lack of food. There are no live, green plants for a marmot to eat in winter, so it hibernates. It slows its heart rate, lowers its body temperature, and goes into an unusually deep sleep. The marmot doesn't eat while it hibernates, so it doesn't need to poop. Instead of eating, a hibernating marmot burns up body fat. This way, it gets all the energy it needs to sleep through the cold winter months. Would you like to sleep all winter long?

Did you know . . .

That SOCKEYE SALMON,
those sleek, slippery, silvery fish,
rot while they are still alive?

Eeewww!!
That's
Yucky!

But hey, it's okay.

Just imagine if it weren't that way!

If it weren't that way, baby salmon would not have good food to eat. Sockeye salmon are born in freshwater streams, but they live most of their lives in the ocean. Adult salmon return to the exact stream where they were born to lay their eggs and fertilize them. Then their skin immediately starts to rot, and they start to die. Their rotting bodies become rich food for river insects. And when the salmon babies hatch, they eat the insects. Do you think river insects sound like yummy baby food?

Did you know . . .
That GREAT GRAY OWLS,
those sharp-eared, secretive, silent hunters,
throw up every day?

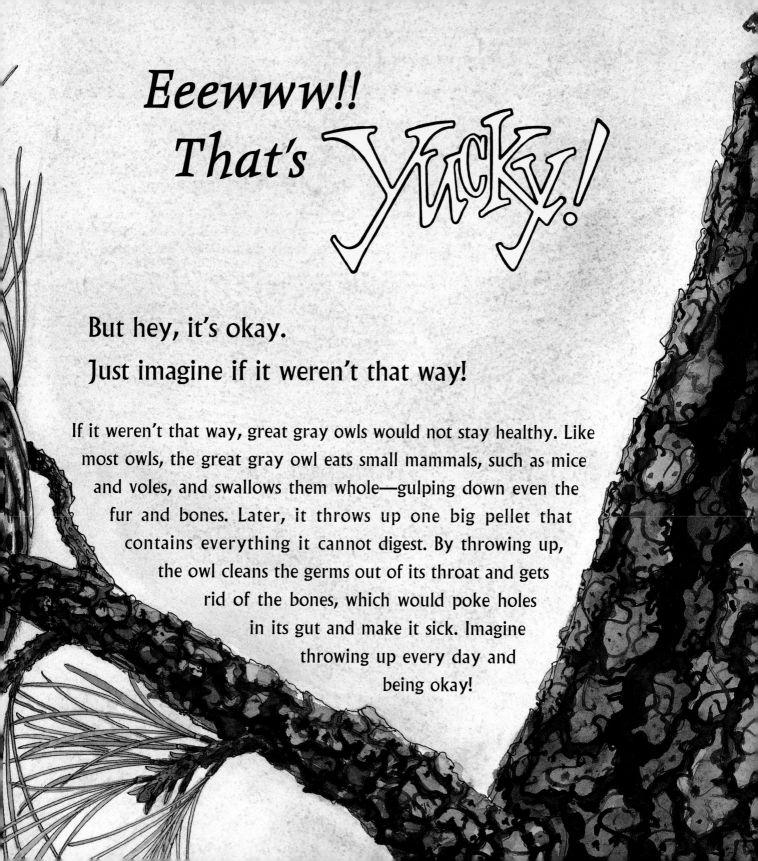

Eeewww!! That's Yucky!

But hey, it's okay.

Just imagine if it weren't that way!

If it weren't that way, great gray owls would not stay healthy. Like most owls, the great gray owl eats small mammals, such as mice and voles, and swallows them whole—gulping down even the fur and bones. Later, it throws up one big pellet that contains everything it cannot digest. By throwing up, the owl cleans the germs out of its throat and gets rid of the bones, which would poke holes in its gut and make it sick. Imagine throwing up every day and being okay!

Did you know . . .

That GRIZZLY BEARS,

those dirt-digging, hump-backed, hulking beasts,

eat rotting meat?

Eeewww!!
That's Yucky!

But hey, it's okay.

Just imagine if it weren't that way!

If it weren't that way, grizzlies would have to hunt more often for food. Grizzlies mainly eat plants, but they also kill animals such as young moose or deer. They can't eat such large animals all at once, so they save the leftovers by covering them with soil. The bears return later to this stashed food, called a cache (say CASH), to munch on the meat—even if it is three days old and really smelly. Grizzly bear mothers could brag that their cubs aren't fussy eaters. Can your mom say that about you?

Did you know . . .
That **HONEYBEES,**
those busy bunches of flower-sipping sisters,
throw up after eating nectar?

Eeewww!! That's Yucky!

But hey, it's okay.

Just imagine if it weren't that way!

If it weren't that way, there would be no honey in the world. Honeybees drink the sweet, sugary liquid, called nectar, that flowers make. The bees don't have bottles to carry the nectar, so they swallow it. Back in the hive, they throw it back up. Then they fan the nectar with their wings and turn it into honey, which they eat during the winter. Next time you eat a honey-sweetened snack, thank the bees for this delicious bee-barf treat!

Did you know . . .
That **TURKEY VULTURES**, those soaring, swooping scavengers, poop on their very own legs?

Eeewww!! That's Yucky!

But hey, it's okay.

Just imagine if it weren't that way!

If it weren't that way, turkey vultures couldn't easily cool themselves. When you need to cool off on a hot day, you might squirt yourself with a hose or run through the sprinklers. When a turkey vulture needs to cool off, it poops on its legs. The vulture's poop is watery. As the water in the poop evaporates, it cools the bird's body—in the same way you feel cool as the water evaporates off your body. Aren't you glad you don't have to poop on yourself to stay cool?

Did you know . . .

That MOUNTAIN LIONS,

those sleek, slinky, stalking cats,

lick their babies' rear ends to make them poop?

Eeewww!!
That's
Yucky!

But hey, it's okay.
Just imagine if it weren't that way!

If it weren't that way, the just-born kittens could not poop or pee. Very young baby mammals are helpless and need a lot of care from their parents. They drink milk from their mother for weeks while their eyes open and their fur grows. Baby mountain lions are so helpless that their mother has to lick their bottoms to get the babies to poop and pee. The mother also eats the waste so the smell doesn't attract enemies. Thank goodness human babies can poop without help!

Did you know . . .

That 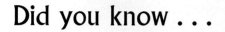 WESTERN PAINTED TURTLES

those colorful-bottomed, cold-blooded critters,

breathe through their butts?

Eeewww!!
That's

YUCKY!

But hey, it's okay.

Just imagine if it weren't that way!

If it weren't that way, these hard-shelled reptiles could not survive freezing-cold weather. During winter, a western painted turtle rests on the muck at the bottom of a shallow lake, stream, or marsh to hibernate for months. It needs to breathe, but ice blocks its way to the air. Under the ice, the turtle can't breathe with its nose, mouth, or lungs, and it doesn't have gills like a fish does. So the turtle absorbs oxygen from the water through special skin in its throat and in the opening in its butt, called the cloaca (say cloh-AY-kuh). That's how a turtle breathes while it hibernates. Bet you can't breathe through your skin!

Did you know . . .

That HERRING GULLS,

those graceful, gliding gobblers of fish,

throw up food for their young?

Eeewww!!
That's Yucky!

But hey, it's okay.

Just imagine if it weren't that way!

If it weren't that way, herring gulls could not feed their babies. These birds don't have pouches like pelicans do for carrying the fish, sea worms, sea stars, and other animals they eat. So gulls swallow their food and throw up the half-digested meal on the floor of the nest for their babies to eat. The hungry young birds eagerly swallow this healthy feast. Aren't you glad your parents don't serve you already-been-eaten food?

Did you know . . .
That GRAY WOLVES,
those powerful, prowling predators,
pee on trees?

Eeewww!! That's Yucky!

But hey, it's okay.

Just imagine if it weren't that way!

If it weren't that way, these relatives of dogs wouldn't be able to tell other wolves to stay away from their territory. Wolves live and hunt in groups called packs. Each pack marks its hunting grounds with strong-smelling pee—it's one way wolves "talk" to other wolves. When wolves from other packs smell the pee, they know a pack already lives and hunts there, so they stay away. That leaves enough food for the pack that lives there. If you tried this in your room, people might stay away, but a "Keep Out" sign might be better.

Did you know . . .

That **SEA STARS,**

those bumpy, bizarre, many-legged crawlers,

put their stomachs outside

their bodies to eat?

Eeewww!! That's  Yucky!

But hey, it's okay.

Just imagine if it weren't that way!

If it weren't that way, they couldn't eat clams, their favorite food. Most sea stars, or starfish, have five legs covered with suction cups called tube feet. To catch its dinner, a sea star crawls over to a clam, covers the clam with its powerful feet, and starts to pull it open. As the sea star begins to open the clam, it pushes its stomach, which looks like a plastic bag, into the crack between the two shells. The stomach makes acidic juices that digest the clam inside its own shell! The sea star then absorbs the gooey clam meat, pulls its stomach back in, and leaves the empty shells behind. Don't try this at home!

Did you know . . .

That **AMERICAN ROBINS,**

those worm-gulping,

sign-of-spring singers,

carry poop in

their mouths?

*Eeewww!!
That's*

Yucky!

But hey, it's okay.

Just imagine if it weren't that way!

If it weren't that way, baby robins would live in a poopy nest and could get sick. You probably eat three or four times each day, but baby robins eat all day long. All the waste from that food comes out the other end and right into the mud-lined nest. The parent birds use their beaks to carry things the way we use our hands. So they grab the tidy bags of poop, called fecal sacs, in their beaks and carry them away. Isn't this natural diaper better than a nest full of poop?

Did you know . . .

That ORCAS,

those furless, fearless, friendly-looking sea creatures,

rip up seals and eat them alive?

Eeewww!!
That's Yucky!

But hey, it's okay.

Just imagine if it weren't that way!

If it weren't that way, their food would be too big to swallow. You've probably been told many times to chew your food well. Orcas, also called killer whales, aren't built to chew their food at all. They hunt for food in family groups called pods. The members of a pod work together to herd their prey into a small area before they all attack. The orcas grab their sea-animal meal, then shake it apart into bite-size pieces. Aren't you glad you can cut and chew your food?

Did you know . . .

That **SNOWSHOE HARES,**

those forest-dwelling, furry-footed hip-hoppers,

eat their own poop?

Eeewww!!
That's

Yucky!

But hey, it's okay.

Just imagine if it weren't that way!

If it weren't that way, they might not get enough food in winter, when there are only twigs and bark to eat. Hares and rabbits make two kinds of poop: soft droppings and sawdusty ones. Their soft droppings still have nutrients in them, so the rabbits eat them. When they poop again, they leave behind sawdusty droppings, which have no food energy left in them. By eating food twice, they get more of the nutrition they need when vitamin-rich leaves are hard to find. It's really too yucky to even think about, but hares and rabbits don't seem to mind!

More about NATURE'S Yucky! ANIMALS

MOOSE *Alces alces*

These largest members of the deer family weigh as much as 1,200 pounds. Moose eat the leaves of many shrubs and trees, and they're also fond of water lilies. In the winter, they eat twigs, which are hard to digest and don't have much food energy. These odd-looking beasts have a bulgy nose; long, knobby legs; a humped shoulder; and large, palmlike antlers. In North America, moose live in the Great Lakes states, the Rocky Mountains, Canada, and Alaska. Bull moose, like other male members of the deer family, use their antlers to fight other moose over breeding rights.

BALD EAGLE *Haliaeetus leucocephalus*

Pesticides, shooting, and habitat destruction almost killed all the bald eagles in the United States. But the banning of the pesticide DDT and better enforcement of poaching laws have allowed bald eagle populations to recover. They are no longer listed as an endangered species. The largest birds of prey in North America, bald eagles now live across most of this continent. Besides their main diet of live and dead fish, eagles also eat muskrats, squirrels, rabbits, injured ducks, and other dead animals. Their treetop stick nests are as large as bathtubs. Eagles can live to be as old as forty-eight years in captivity.

HOARY MARMOT *Marmota caligata*

Marmots live in the mountains of the Cascade Range and the northern Rocky Mountains in the United States and Canada. The summers there are very short, so marmots may hibernate for eight months—that's longer than they are awake! During hibernation, their bodies burn just enough body fat to keep them alive. In the short summer, they pig out on many kinds of green plants. Their nickname "whistle pig" comes from the sharp whistle they make when alarmed. Hoary marmots commonly live in colonies and build complex tunnel systems under boulder fields.

SOCKEYE SALMON *Oncorhynchus nerka*

Commonly called red salmon, these amazing fish live in freshwater streams and rivers for one to three years. Then they live for one to four years in the Pacific and Arctic Oceans and use their sense of smell to find their way back to the same stream in which they were born. They can even jump up a waterfall to get there. Sockeye salmon are silvery when living in the ocean, but when they prepare to breed, both the males and females turn mostly red and their heads and tails turn olive green. Males will fight, bite, and bash each other to get access to the courting females. In some regions, large hydroelectric dams and pollution threaten salmon's ability to get to the ocean to grow up, and to go upriver to their breeding grounds.

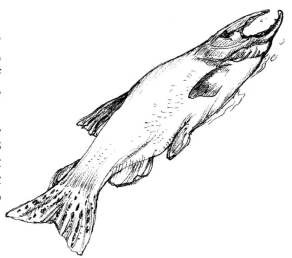

GREAT GRAY OWL *Strix nebulosa*

Great gray owls are the largest, but not the heaviest, owls in North America. They live year-round in conifer forests of central Alaska, the Yukon, and Ontario, and in the forested mountains of California, Oregon, Washington, Idaho, Montana, and northern Minnesota. In hard winters, they migrate south to the snowy northern areas of Wisconsin and the Upper Peninsula of Michigan. Unlike most other owls, great grays sometimes hunt during the day. They eat voles, mice, shrews, rats, gophers, rabbits, hares, red squirrels, and occasionally small birds. Owls roost, or hang out, in a favorite tree when they are not hunting. That is generally where they cough up their pellets. Scientists look for pellets under roost trees, then pick apart the pellets to find out exactly what the owls have eaten. You'll know a boreal forest is healthy if a great gray owl lives there.

GRIZZLY BEAR *Ursus arctos*

When Lewis and Clark were exploring the West, 50,000 to 100,000 grizzly bears roamed what is now the continental United States. Today only about 1,000 grizzlies live in the lower forty-eight states—and those only in the Rocky Mountain states. Grizzly bears need large, wild areas in which to live. Habitat destruction, hunting, and human encroachment into wild places are the main reasons grizzly populations have declined. Also called brown bears, these extremely powerful predators eat mainly roots, berries, leaves, and grass. In fact, 98 percent of their diet comes from plants. During the long winter, grizzlies, like other North American bears, hibernate in dens. While hibernating, grizzlies burn their body fat for energy and keep warm in their heavy fur coats.

HONEYBEE *Apis mellifera*

Unlike wasp nests, honeybee hives remain active in winter. But there are no blooming flowers in most of the United States during the winter, and bees cannot go outside their hives in below-freezing temperatures. So, they eat the stored honey they made from the nectar that worker bees, which all are female, collected during the warm months. Honeybees communicate by movement, called bee dances, to tell each other where to find blooming flowers. Only the female worker bees have stingers. Unlike wasps, bees die if they sting something. Commercial honeybees originally came from Europe. Besides making honey, bees pollinate many types of fruits and vegetables as they unwittingly carry pollen from flower to flower. People use beeswax, honey, and bee pollen in many products, including candles, cosmetics, flavoring for food and drink, and health food supplements.

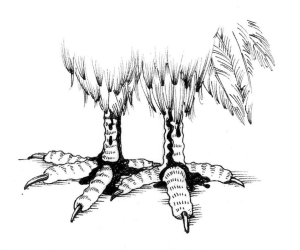

TURKEY VULTURE *Cathartes aura*

Sometimes called buzzards, turkey vultures live throughout the United States. These superb gliders and flyers hop clumsily when on the ground. Although they eat mainly carrion—both freshly dead animals and really rotten ones—they sometimes kill and eat baby herons, pigs, grasshoppers, and fish. Vultures are one of the few birds proven to have a keen sense of smell, which makes them one of nature's great cleanup machines—picking at carcasses until very little is left. One vulture lived to be twenty years old in a zoo. Vultures have nearly bald heads, which are easier for the birds to keep clean and free of parasites.

MOUNTAIN LION *Felis concolor*

Also known as pumas, panthers, and cougars, mountain lions historically lived throughout North and South America. In the United States, they now live mainly in the West and in the Gulf states, and are sporadically sighted in Maine and the southern Appalachian Mountains. Mountain lions need lots of space away from people in which to hunt. They hunt night or day, primarily for deer. Females usually have two or three kittens in spring. They live in mountains, forests, and deserts. Mountain lions are not fast runners. To hunt, they stalk their prey or wait for the prey to come within 50 to 100 feet and then pounce on it.

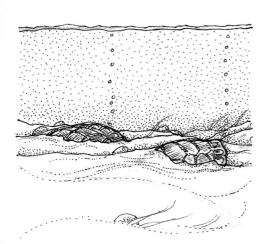

WESTERN PAINTED TURTLE *Chrysemys picta bellii*

Western painted turtles are larger than the two eastern subspecies of painted turtles and have the most intricate yellow line patterns on their bottom shells, called plastrons. Males have concave bottom shells and very long front claws. Western painted turtles live in soft-bottomed, shallow waters, such as lakes, ponds, marshes, streams, and even ditches. They eat water plants, water insects, snails, and crayfish. Turtle populations have suffered from loss of habitat, being run over by cars, and raccoons eating their eggs. They should never be collected from the wild as pets.

HERRING GULL *Larus argentatus*

Herring gulls live over all of North America and even in northern Canada during the summer. They are one of the largest gulls, weighing up to 2½ pounds. Gulls mainly eat a lot of dead animals and are great "garbage collectors" for the beaches and harbors. They also eat small fish, sea urchins, sea stars, shellfish, eggs, baby birds, mice, beetles, and wasps. Herring gulls catch small fish from the surface of lakes, streams, and the ocean. Gulls can break open and eat clams and crabs by dropping them onto rocks or pavement from high in the air. They have also learned that human activities provide them with food. Gulls look for food at garbage dumps, follow farmers' plows that bring up worms in fields, and circle fishing boats to scavenge dumped fish parts.

GRAY WOLF   *Canis lupus*

Gray wolves, also known as timber wolves, once lived across most of North America and also in Europe. Gray wolves are sacred to some Native American people. Settlers hunted the wolves to near extinction in the 1800s, and until recently gray wolves survived only in Canada, Alaska, and Minnesota. Gray wolves are now expanding their range into Wisconsin, Michigan, Idaho, Montana, and Wyoming. These large members of the canid, or dog, family weigh as much as 130 pounds. Because they are large animals that live in family groups, or packs, of typically five to eight animals, wolves can catch and kill moose and deer, their main food. They also eat beavers, mice, hares, waterfowl, and even salmon.

SEA STAR   class Asteroidea, thousands of species

Commonly called starfish, sea stars are not fish at all! They belong to an unusual group of animals called echinoderms (say ih-KY-nuh-dermz), which means "bumpy skin." Sea stars live around the world in the shallows of oceans—on coral, rocks, and piers. They are usually orange but can also be pale green, blue, purple, cream, or dark red. Some are even spotted. Sea stars and their cousins—sea urchins, sand dollars, and sea cucumbers—typically have a five-parted body and tube feet that look like suction cups. They use their feet to move around, hang onto the rocky bottom, and catch their food. Sea stars are slow movers that can travel up to 6 inches per minute. They have no head or eyes. They eat urchins, fish, crabs, shrimp, clams, and coral polyps. If a sea star's "arm" is cut off, it can grow another one.

AMERICAN ROBIN   *Turdus migratorius*

These well-known and common birds breed in all of North America except near the Arctic Ocean. They are the state birds of three states: Connecticut, Michigan, and Wisconsin. Robins live in forests, mountains up to treeline, orchards, and pastures, and they flourish in city parks and suburban yards. Watch for them hopping or walking in short grass as they look for earthworms. They also eat beetles, grasshoppers, caterpillars, crabapples, grapes, and many kinds of berries. Robins make their grass-and-mud nests in forked tree branches as well as on buildings. They lay beautiful aqua blue eggs and can raise multiple families in one season. The fecal sacs that the baby robins produce are whitish, gelatinous pouches that contain their poop and pee. Robins are beloved signs of spring. They arrive back in the northern half of the continent in March, even before all the snow melts.

ORCA   *Orcinus orca*

Orcas, also known as killer whales, are not true whales but rather the largest member of the dolphin family *(Delphinidae)*. They can be 30 feet long and weigh 10 tons. Around North America, orcas live in the Arctic and northern Pacific Oceans. Males have a long dorsal, or back, fin up to nearly 6 feet tall, while females sport fins less than 3 feet tall. This "wolf of the sea" eats fish (cod, halibut, sardines, salmon, and tuna), seals, sharks, octopus, other dolphins, sea otters, and sometimes smaller whales. They travel and live in groups, called pods, of usually a few to as many as thirty individuals. One pod had 150 orcas!

SNOWSHOE HARE   *Lepus americanus*

This rabbit relative wears a different-colored coat in winter than in summer. In winter, snowshoe hares are white to blend with the snow. In summer, they are grayish brown to blend with the forest floor. Populations of snowshoe hares fluctuate widely, typically in ten-year cycles. Populations of predators, such as lynx, that eat mainly hares also swing wildly as the availability of their food increases and decreases. Hares eat plants, grasses, leaves, and buds in the summer and browse on twigs in the winter. Their name comes from the large toes and coarse, stiff hair on their hind feet, which, like snowshoes, allow them to move easily over deep snow.

Scat Cookies

Naturalists call animal poop "scat." Here's a delicious way to learn about animal scat. Follow this recipe—or find a ready-made chocolate chocolate-chip cookie mix in the store—and make cookies shaped like mammal scat. Feed them to your friends after telling them some interesting facts you've learned from reading *Nature's Yucky!* And if you really want to impress people, call them "Coprophagy Cookies," after the term for animals that eat their own droppings for extra energy!

We recommend using as many organic ingredients as possible. When fewer pesticides are used in growing food, animals and their environment benefit—and people do, too!

Scat cookies ready to go into the oven: 1) bear, 2) wolf, 3) mountain lion, 4) snowshoe hare (enlarged so as not to burn).

Grandparents and their grandchildren make scat cookies at the Wood Lake Nature Center in Richfield, Minnesota.

SCAT COOKIES

Ingredients

1 cup butter, softened

1½ cups white sugar

2 eggs

2 teaspoons vanilla extract

2 cups all-purpose flour

⅔ cup cocoa powder

¾ teaspoon baking soda

¼ teaspoon salt

1 cup semisweet chocolate chips

1 cup peanut butter chips

Directions

1. Preheat oven to 350° F

2. In a large bowl, beat butter, sugar, eggs, and vanilla until light and fluffy. In a separate bowl, combine the flour, cocoa, baking soda, and salt. Stir the flour mixture into the butter mixture until well blended. Mix in the chocolate and peanut butter chips.

3. Lightly butter your hands. Roll the dough into scat shapes. Place smaller, rounded scat cookies, such as rabbit scat, on one cookie sheet and larger, rolled and twisted scat cookies, such as mountain lion scat, on another cookie sheet. That way you can bake the two sheets for different lengths of time if needed.

4. Bake for 8 to 10 minutes, keeping an eye on the smaller scat cookies so they don't burn.

Happy scat snacking!

About the Authors

Both Lee Ann Landstrom and Karen I. Shragg are longtime educators of children and adults. Landstrom directs the Eastman Nature Center for the Three Rivers Parks District in Osseo, Minnesota. She has a master's degree in biology, is a past president of the Minnesota Association for Environmental Education, and served for many years on the board of the Minnesota Naturalists' Association. Shragg heads the Wood Lake Nature Center in Richfield, Minnesota. She has a master's degree in outdoor education and recreation and a doctorate in education. She has written another children's book, *A Solstice Tree for Jenny,* and co-edited *Tree Stories: A Collection of Extraordinary Encounters.*

About the Illustrator

Constance Bergum is a Montana native and has been a designer and illustrator of children's books for the past seventeen years. She holds a B.A. in art from the University of Montana and an M.F.A. in illustration from Marywood University. Her numerous awards include the Washington Writers Award for *Seya's Song* and the Ezra Jack Keats Fellowship. *Nature's Yucky!* is her seventh picture book for children. She lives in Helena, Montana, with her husband, Ron, and three children, William, Elizabeth, and Sophie.

We encourage you to patronize your local bookstore. Most stores will order any title that they do not stock. You may also order directly from Mountain Press using the order form provided below or by calling our toll-free number and using your credit card. We will gladly send you a catalog upon request.

YOUNG ADULT

_____ *Bold Women in Michigan's History*	*paper/$12.00*
_____*Crazy Horse: A Photographic Biography*	*paper/$20.00*
_____*Custer: A Photographic Biography*	*paper/$24.00*
_____*Lewis and Clark: A Photographic Journey*	*paper/$18.00*
_____*The Oregon Trail: A Photographic Journey*	*paper/$18.00*
_____*The Pony Express: A Photographic History*	*paper/$22.00*
_____*Sacagawea's Son: The Life of Jean Baptiste Charbonneau*	*paper/$10.00*
_____*Smoky: The Cowhorse*	*paper/$16.00*
_____*Stories of Young Pioneers: In Their Own Words*	*paper/$14.00*

CHILDREN

_____*Awesome Osprey: Fishing Birds of the World*	*paper/$12.00*
_____*The Charcoal Forest: How Fire Helps Animals and Plants*	*paper/$12.00*
_____*Cowboy in the Making*	*cloth/$15.00*
_____*Glacier National Park: An ABC Adventure*	*paper/$10.00*
_____*Loons: Diving Birds of the North*	*paper/$12.00*
_____*My First Horse*	*paper/$16.00*
_____*Nature's Yucky! Gross Stuff That Helps Nature Work*	*paper/$10.00*
_____*Nature's Yucky 2! The Desert Southwest*	*paper/$12.00*
_____*Owls: Whoo Are They?*	*paper/$12.00*
_____*Snowy Owls: Whoo Are They?*	*cloth/$12.00*
_____*Spotted Bear: A Rocky Mountain Folktale*	*cloth/$15.00*
_____*The Will James Cowboy Book*	*cloth/$18.00*
_____*You Can Be a Nature Detective*	*paper/$14.00*
_____*Young Cowboy*	*cloth/$15.00*

Please include $3.00 for 1-4 books or $5.00 for 5 or more books for shipping and handling.

Send the books marked above. I enclose $ _____

Name _____

Address_____

City/State/Zip _____

☐ Payment enclosed (check or money order in U.S. funds)

Bill my: ☐ VISA ☐ MasterCard ☐ American Express ☐ Discover

Card No. _____ Exp. Date:_____

Security Code #_____Signature _____

MP Mountain Press
PUBLISHING COMPANY
P.O. Box 2399 • Missoula, MT 59806 • 406-728-1900
800-234-5308 • info@mtnpress.com
www.mountain-press.com